THE BALTIC STATES

by
Gail B. Stewart

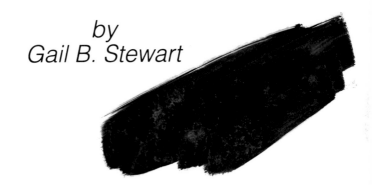

CRESTWOOD HOUSE
New York

Maxwell Macmillan Canada
Toronto

Maxwell Macmillan International
New York Oxford Singapore Sydney

Library of Congress Cataloging-in-Publication Data
Stewart, Gail, 1949–
    The Baltic States / by Gail B. Stewart
        p.   cm. — (Places in the news)
    Includes index.
    Summary: Discusses the history and present status of Lithuania, Latvia, and Estonia.
    ISBN 0-89686-747-1
    1. Baltic States—History—Juvenile literature. [1. Baltic States—History.] I. Title. II. Series: Stewart, Gail, 1949–
Places in the news.
DK502.7.S84   1992
947'.04—dc20

92-40
CIP
AC

Photo Credits
Cover: AP—Wide World Photos
AP—Wide World Photos: 4, 7, 8, 17, 25, 29, 30, 33, 34, 36, 37, 38, 39, 40, 41, 44
The Bettmann Archive: 13, 19, 21

CRESTWOOD HOUSE

Macmillan Publishing Company
866 Third Avenue
New York, NY 10022

Maxwell Macmillan Canada, Inc.
1200 Eglinton Avenue East
Suite 200
Don Mills, Ontario M3C 3N1

Macmillan Publishing Company is part of the Maxwell Communication Group of Companies.

Produced by Flying Fish Studio

Printed in the United States of America

First Edition

10 9 8 7 6 5 4 3 2 1

CONTENTS

THE BALTICS IN THE NEWS

During August 1991, the world's attention was focused on the Soviet Union. Top Soviet leaders directed a coup, a forceful change in the government. These leaders had disagreed with the way Mikhail Gorbachev had been running the country. They wanted the Soviet Union to follow the ideas of communism more strictly.

By August 21 the coup was over. Gorbachev was restored to power and hard-line Communist officials were jailed. With the "troublemakers" out of the way and their leader back in the Kremlin, would the Soviet Union continue as before?

"A New Period in History"

It did not take long for people around the world to understand that the Soviet Union had changed. On Wednesday, August 21, within hours of the coup's end, three Soviet states declared their independence. Estonia, Latvia and Lithuania—known as the Baltic states—said that they no longer wanted to be part of the Soviet Union.

Ordered by coup leaders, Soviet tanks head for Moscow to crush the movement for freedom and reform.

Their insistence was nothing new. They had been asking for their freedom for years. The news was that this time Gorbachev was willing to give it to them.

In a speech to the Soviet people, Gorbachev said, "If independence is the final wish and intention of the people of the Baltics, then I think we must agree to it."

Vytautas Landsbergis, the president of Lithuania, was pleased at the news of Gorbachev's decision. During a rally at Vilnius, the capital of Lithuania, President Landsbergis said, "I am glad that he has said this. This is the beginning of a new period of history."

The Unraveling of an Empire

Letting go of the Baltics was a big step for the Soviet Union. Many political experts around the world saw the event as the beginning of the end of the Soviets.

"The Soviet Union is a huge, 15-piece collection of stolen property," wrote one newspaper. "Sooner or later it was bound to happen. It seems as though now is the time to return the seized states to their rightful owners."

The Baltic states were not the only piece of the Soviet "collection" that wished to be independent. The Ukraine, Moldavia, Byelorussia, Georgia and Kazakhstan all indicated that they too were aiming to be free.

"This empire that we live in is becoming unglued," said a woman from Latvia. "Perhaps, as they say, we Balts are the ones who began the whole thing. But we are not the only ones. This is a huge nation, the Soviet Empire. The Communist leaders can no longer force so many people to think as one."

Political experts have various ideas of what will happen to the Soviet Union in the next years. But one thing they all agree on is that the huge nation will be forever changed. It is simply too large an empire to stay together. There are more than 300 million people, and the territory is so large that it spans 11 different time zones! Even without political differences it would be almost impossible to keep such a large country unified.

Many Ways of Celebrating

During the autumn of 1991, the people of the Baltic states were not concerned with the entire Soviet Union. They were interested in looking ahead to the future of the Baltics. And they were happy to be able to celebrate their new freedom. That celebration took on many different forms.

Young children touch the toppled statue of Lenin.

In Lithuania's capital, more than 20,000 people gathered at a victory rally. Thousands cheered as a large iron statue of former Soviet leader Vladimir Ilyich Lenin was pushed over. Many climbed over the toppled statue, yelling, "We are not Soviet citizens!" and "Lenin was not our hero!"

One young woman shredded a large red-and-yellow Soviet flag that had been waving over the center of the city. "I see no reason for that flag to be here," she explained to the newspeople. "The colors that we love are the red, green and yellow of our own flag."

A member of the Black Berets leaves Latvia.

The celebrations were less festive in Riga, the capital of Latvia. There, special Soviet soldiers were climbing onto jeeps and trucks that would take them back to Moscow. The soldiers, part of a highly trained team known as the Black Berets, had been in Latvia for over a year. Their job had been to intimidate and harass Latvians working for freedom.

But in September 1991, the soldiers were leaving, and many Latvian people gathered to watch them go. Some people taunted the soldiers, whistling and waving Latvian flags.

The soldiers were angry that they were being recalled. They felt that they were heroes and should not have to leave the Baltics as if they had been beaten. The soldiers shouted insults back at the crowd and put up a large sign in red letters on one of their jeeps. The sign read WE WILL RETURN. As the soldiers left, their jeeps swerved close to the crowds, as if to run them down.

Some Balts found less public ways to celebrate their freedom. One woman who worked as an economics expert in Lithuania pulled a little bottle of whiskey from her bottom drawer. "I have been keeping this for a very long time, for a special occasion," she said, smiling. "Now is the time to have a taste."

"But Winter Is Coming"

But as much as the Baltic people were rejoicing in their independence, they were concerned about their future.

"It is not the future of the Soviet Union that we worry about," says a teacher from Lithuania. "That is a large superhighway. Our future, like that of the Estonians and that of the Latvians, is a little path. We need to worry about where the path leads. Do we have enough jobs to keep our people busy and prosperous? Will we be able to trade as equal partners with the nations of Europe?

9

"These are the things that concern us today, even as we celebrate, even as we wave our flags and cry with joy. There is so much we need to do, and so much we need to prove to ourselves."

Government leaders in the Baltic states agree. They know, for instance, that they cannot provide fuel for their own nations. They have, in the past, bought their energy from the Soviet Union, at a very minimal price. However, since they no longer are part of the Soviet Union, they worry that the price now will be more than they can afford. How will they heat their homes and businesses without a good supply of fuel?

"I love freedom, I love the taste of it and the sound," says a 76-year-old grandfather from Estonia. "But winter is coming, and it gets cold here. I can remember a time when we used to be free and we needed no one but ourselves. But that was before the Soviets. We need to learn again how to think like a free country and not a state dependent on the handouts of others to survive."

But political experts in the United States expect that the little nations will need help, at least for a while.

"They're going to be like all small, poor, weak countries out there," says an American government official who has studied the Baltics. "They're going to be dependent upon outside powers for their survival."

How did the Baltic states—once free nations—come to be part of the Soviet Empire? How did Soviet rule affect them? And what was so terrible that they risked their lives to become free once again?

A HISTORY OF DOMINATION

The challenges that face the people of the Baltics are very current. They have had very little practice in being free. The only time these nations were independent was from 1918 to 1940! Since their beginnings many hundreds of years ago, Estonia, Latvia and Lithuania have been controlled by outsiders.

Much-Desired Territory

People have lived in the area known as the Baltics for thousands of years. Archaeologists are scientists who study ancient civilizations. They have found evidence that there were people living in Estonia, Latvia and Lithuania as long ago as 8000 B.C.

No one knows very much about these people—only that they were run off by other people at about the time of Christ. These newcomers were the long-ago ancestors of today's Balts.

The Baltic lands, so called because they lie next to the Baltic Sea, have always been desirable. The land is lush and green, with beautiful, ancient forests. The soil is fertile, and because of the land's closeness to the sea, the temperature is milder than in much of the rest of the Soviet Union.

The ancient Baltic people had no national boundaries. They lived in large tribes, with a king or chief who was elected by the people. The Balts were farmers and trappers. Some were woodsmen; others harvested amber, a beautiful brownish yellow mineral used in jewelry. A Roman historian wrote in A.D. 100 about the Baltic people who sold excellent quality amber to Roman traders.

The nations of Estonia, Lithuania and Latvia were created around 1100. Individual tribes united to give themselves more security against outsiders. They formed boundaries of three separate nations and established trade with other countries.

The Teutonic Knights

But even with their new, large nations, the Baltic people were always in danger. From the 1200s on, they were bombarded by a variety of nations and tribes.

The Teutonic Knights ruled with the sword.

In the 1200s all three nations were attacked by a group called the Teutonic Knights. This was an organization that was both military and religious. It was made up of Germans who believed it was their duty as Christians to spread their religion to other people. Even if it meant killing entire villages and burning towns, they believed God was on their side. The Teutonic Knights were able to convert the Baltic people to Christianity in this forceful, violent way.

Besides controlling the religions of the Baltic people, the Teutonic Knights had a major effect on the economy and lifestyle of the people. Instead of the land being owned by Baltic people, it was owned by wealthy German nobles. The nobles employed Balts to work on their farms, but the Balts were treated poorly.

By the 1300s the Teutonic Knights were no longer a controlling religious force in the Baltics. However, the German landowners remained. They continued to keep the land as their own, handing it down from father to son.

Fighting for Survival

In the centuries that followed, ownership of the Baltic states changed several times. The three nations were sought after for a number of reasons. They all had resources that were desirable— timber, amber and rich farmland. They were strategically important too. All of them could provide the conquering nations with warm-water ports on the Baltic Sea. Finally, the nations were small enough for the hungry empires of Europe to take over fairly easily.

Sweden, Poland, Denmark and Germany all took turns conquering the Baltic people and establishing control there. Each of the conquering armies left its mark on the Baltic states. Language, culture and the government changed to reflect the "owners" of Latvia, Estonia and Lithuania.

But one aspect of Baltic life remained the same—the land continued to be held by wealthy German nobles. And the Balts continued to be serfs—poor peasants who depended on the landowners for their survival. In exchange for working as servants and farmers on the noble's land, each serf got a tiny hut to live in and a small share of the crops grown. Serfs had no power—they could not vote or be represented. They were virtually slaves in their own country.

Part of the Russian Empire

During the 18th and 19th centuries, another world power was hungry for more land. Russia (the name of the Soviet Union before 1922) was sending its armies into central Europe. The Russian czar, or king, was anxious to increase the size of his empire.

In 1720 Estonia, Latvia and Lithuania fell to the Russian army. For the next 100 years, these countries were controlled by Russia.

There were many Baltic people who resented the Russians. It angered them that they could not fight the Russians and drive them out of their lands. The Lithuanians tried to rebel in 1831 and again in 1863, but they failed. The czar's armies were too powerful.

The Baltic people fought in other ways, though. They worked very hard to educate their children. They kept their culture and their language alive. They believed that as long as their heritage and customs existed, then a part of them would be free.

But the czar was unwilling to allow the parts of his empire to keep their separate identities. He wanted them to be Russian—to follow Russian customs and to speak the Russian language. He sent orders to Lithuania, after the uprisings there, that all schools be closed. He made a law that said it was illegal to sell or read books in the Lithuanian language.

Many Baltic families moved to the United States during this time. Even though they had neither savings nor jobs waiting for them, they chose to take a chance on a free life in the United States. Others who stayed in the Baltics tried to continue their language studies and cultural education in secret.

Independence— for a Short While

By the end of the 19th century there was a growing movement in Estonia, Latvia and Lithuania for independence. As Russia and Germany (which still had large holdings of land in the Baltics) became distracted with the growing problems in Europe, the Baltic people pushed even harder for freedom.

In 1917 it seemed for a short time as though their prayers would be answered. A large uprising had occurred in Russia— people had risen up against the czar and his armies. The new Communist government was led by Vladimir Ilyich Lenin. Lenin believed, as did other Communists, that the common people should make decisions about their own lives. He thought it was wrong for czars and wealthy people to run the country.

16

Vladimir Ilyich Lenin

17

Lenin announced right away that the non-Russian parts of the empire should have the right to decide whether they wished to remain part of Russia or if they would choose to be self-governing. It sounded to the people of Estonia, Latvia and Lithuania as if they finally had an ally.

But their excitement was brief. Lenin was surprised to learn that most of the non-Russian republics wanted to take him up on his offer. Like the Baltic states, they were eager to become independent.

Lenin could not allow the bulk of his empire to break away. Instead, he sent his armies into the various republics to use strong-arm tactics. People who organized rallies and independence plans were shot or jailed. Anyone who went against the wishes of Lenin and his armies was considered an enemy of Russia and was dealt with accordingly.

There were so many "enemies" for Lenin to fight that he could not control them all. The Russians tried to recapture the Baltics, but without success. Estonia, Latvia and Lithuania declared their independence, and by 1920 Russia was forced to accept it.

The Devil's Pact

As free states, the three Baltic nations began running their governments their own way. Each set up a parliament, whose representatives would be elected by the people. They took the large estates, owned by German nobles since the Middle Ages, and divided them into small farms. These were distributed to Baltic people.

This time of freedom lasted only two decades. At the same time as the Baltic people were working to help their new nations

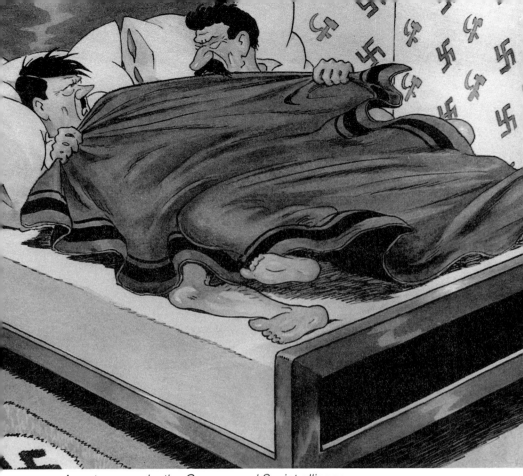

A cartoon mocks the German and Soviet alliance.

grow, a deal was being made. The deal was between two dictators, Adolf Hitler of Germany and Joseph Stalin of the Soviet Union. They were allies, and as they looked at a map of Europe, they had plans to carve it up between themselves.

"It was a true devil's pact," says a Latvian doctor whose father was alive when the bargain was struck. "The two most evil men of the twentieth century were dividing the continent as if it were a steak and they were two hungry dogs. The formal agreement we had with Russia, that assuring our independence, was forgotten."

Indeed, the Baltics were one of the first chunks of Europe to be assigned. Hitler and Stalin agreed that the Soviet Union could have the Baltics. And in the summer of 1940, Soviet troops invaded—first seizing Lithuania.

The Soviets set up a phony government in Vilnius. They held elections but allowed only Communist party candidates to run for office. The newly elected Communist members of the parliament did what Soviet leaders made them do—they voted to make Lithuania a Communist country. The same thing then occurred in Latvia and Estonia.

A Double Cross, and Back Again

There is an old saying that there is "honor among thieves"— that even criminals have a code of loyalty to one another. But this was certainly not the case when the Baltics were seized.

About a year after Stalin's armies had taken the Baltics by force, Hitler went back on his word. His German armies made a surprise attack on the Soviet Union. In June 1941, Germany seized the Baltics. Instead of having a Communist government, the Baltic people were told that they were now part of the *German* Empire, with Hitler as their dictator.

Throughout World War II the Baltics were held by Germany. However, near the end of the war Germany was being soundly attacked by the Allies. Stalin was able to fight back. Russian troops invaded the Baltics and drove the Germans out. When the war ended in 1945, the Soviets were firmly in control.

Once again, after no more than 20 years of freedom, the Baltic states had fallen under the control of another nation. After bouncing from one empire to another, they were again the property of the Soviet Union.

German tanks roll into Lithuania.

THE BALTICS UNDER COMMUNISM

The Baltic people had already had a taste of life under Soviet rule. They were not surprised, then, when Stalin used violence against them in 1945.

The Reign of Terror and the Forest War

It was known as a "reign of terror." Stalin's armies and secret police invaded Estonia, Latvia and Lithuania. Those who were believed to be critics of the Soviets, or who had fought against the invading Soviet armies, were rounded up.

Many thousands were hanged or shot. Hundreds of thousands were arrested and sent to Siberia. Siberia is the coldest, most remote part of the Soviet Union. It was used during Stalin's time as a forced-labor camp. Many who were sent to Siberia were tortured or worked to death.

Historians say that the reign of terror reduced the population of the Baltics drastically. In Lithuania alone, more than one-third of the population was killed or exiled to Siberia!

But many Baltic people fought back. In Lithuania, for instance, thousands of citizens fought a guerrilla war against the Soviet armies. Instead of organizing themselves into regiments like regular armies, guerrilla fighters are far more secret. They wear no special uniforms and they don't march or carry flags. But they find ways to make life miserable for their enemies. Guerrillas bomb tanks and power stations, shoot at patrols and cause damage to roads and bridges.

The guerrillas of Lithuania did their hiding out in caves and forests in the countryside. For that reason, the guerrillas were respectfully known to their fellow Lithuanians as forest brothers. They fought the Soviets in the Baltics until 1952, when they were finally wiped out by the Soviet soldiers.

A New Economic System

One of the first changes in the Baltic states after the takeover had to do with their economic systems. Under the Communist system, things changed a great deal.

Under communism, private ownership was abolished. Communism is based on the idea that private ownership of anything—homes, farms, businesses—leads to inequality. In fact, it is not fair for some to be wealthy and some poor. If the state—meaning all of the people—owns everything, everyone then can share the profits equally. So in the Baltic states, as in the rest of the Soviet Union, there was an end to privately owned farms. There were no longer private businesses and factories. From 1945 on, everything fell under the control of the Communist state.

"They Ruined Our Farms"

The system might have looked all right on paper, but in real life it failed dismally. The neat, orderly family farms of the Baltic people had been very productive before communism. But when they were seized and put under government control, it was nothing short of disaster.

The small farms were combined into large collectives. These were run by government administrators, who decided what to plant and when. Few of these administrators knew anything about farming.

"They ruined our farms," says one man from rural Latvia. "We used to feel pride and responsibility for our land. But the land suddenly was not ours. A farmer must feel love of his land, love of the tasks that must be done. There is no love when it is somebody else's soil.

"In fact, we were no longer even farmers. We were laborers, like factory workers on an assembly line. Some days you till, some you plant. Or you take apart machines and clean the equipment. But you never decide for yourself. It is always the managers who think for you. It is nonsense."

This system of decisions being made by managers instead of by farmers often led to trouble. For instance, the Soviet government in Moscow decided that it needed more wheat production in Estonia.

Administrators decided to create a large collective farm near Tallinn, Estonia's capital. They combined hundreds of small farms and cleared acres of land and dug irrigation ditches. They bulldozed the land so that it was flat, the way wheat fields must be.

Collective farmers on their way to work

However, as many Estonian farmers point out, the government administrators did not look at a map when they made this farm. If they had, they would have seen that the climate near Tallinn was not suitable for growing wheat. The growing season is too short—with wicked spring and autumn frosts that can wipe out entire harvests.

Because of poor planning, the Soviet Union lost a great deal of time and money. And much to the irritation of the Soviet people, the shortage of wheat caused shortages of bread and cereal products all around the country.

Industry and Its Problems

The Soviet system caused damage to the Baltics in other ways. Moscow's government planners needed factories to do heavy industry, so they looked to the Baltic people.

Huge forests were cut down in the 1950s and 1960s to make way for mining and industry. In Estonia, a country that had once been filled with prosperous farms and thriving villages, factories and mines became common. Large housing projects were built for the workers, so that small cities grew around the factories. The rural villages simply disappeared.

And the emphasis on heavy industry in the Baltics caused another problem—pollution. "It's a big problem now," says a professor at a Latvian university. "We never had air this murky. The chemicals run off unchecked, directly into the rivers and streams. Fifty years ago you could drink from that stream. Now that water could kill a horse."

The Baltic people complained that their land was being

ruined. They petitioned the Soviet government to cut back on the time the factories could belch smoke into the air.

But the Soviet government could not oblige them. There was a need for more electrical equipment, for household appliances and automobiles.

"It was a no-win situation," says a government worker in Estonia. "There were shortages of everything, in Moscow, everywhere in the country. People were waiting two, three years for a refrigerator or a car. And even though everyone knew that the air and water were being ruined, the factories had to keep running, sometimes 24 hours a day.

"I guess it was easier to have the Estonians or the Latvians complaining than those in Moscow or other large cities. We were farther away; we had no political power. We really didn't count for much of anything."

Undermining the People

But the Soviets brought more than economic changes to the Baltics. Knowing that the Baltic people loved freedom, the Soviet leaders worried that there might be uprisings in Estonia, Latvia and Lithuania.

Moscow's answer was to weaken the Baltic states. For instance, in 1945 the population of Estonia was 90 percent Estonian. Latvians made up 75 percent of Latvia's population. An overwhelming majority of natives in each state put the Soviets at a disadvantage. The Soviets were always the minority, and even though they had power, they were always wary.

But if they could dilute the population, there would be less risk of large uprisings. That was the idea when the Soviet government began urging Russians to move to the Baltic states.

In many cases, the government offered bribes to Soviet citizens to move. They were given good, high-paying jobs in business and government. And while native Balts had to wait ten years for an apartment to become available, Soviets coming to the Baltics were given apartments right away.

In the years after 1945, the Soviet plan worked. The one-sided majority of Baltic people has been pared down. In Estonia, the 90 percent was trimmed to 60 percent. In Latvia, the 75 percent dropped to just over 50 percent.

The Soviet government interfered in other ways. It forced schools to teach Russian, even though the Baltic people continued to teach their own languages to their children. The Russian language is far different; it even uses a different alphabet.

Religion, too, was worrisome to the Soviet leaders. Like many other Europeans, the people of the Baltic states have strong Christian backgrounds. Catholic and Protestant churches are common.

But communism teaches that loyalty to anyone or anything but the state is wrong—and dangerous. For that reason, Moscow made laws forbidding the teaching of religion. Charity work done by churches was forbidden as well. The Baltic people were allowed to attend worship services, but to do so they were endangering themselves. Those who went to church were usually kept out of good jobs or the finer universities.

An elderly woman lights a candle in a Russian Orthodox church.

Perestroika?

As the years went by, the frustration and anger of the Baltic people grew. But when Mikhail Gorbachev became the Soviet leader in March 1985, things seemed to change.

Gorbachev was more liberal than the leaders who preceded him. He felt that the problems faced by the Soviet Union could no longer be solved by force. He proposed two new ideas for the government—*glasnost* and *perestroika*. *Glasnost* means "openness." Gorbachev wanted to remove the secrecy from the government, and *glasnost* "would open windows to let the light in."

Perestroika means "a restructuring of politics and the economy." Gorbachev hoped that by loosening the strict rules of communism a little, he would encourage workers to be more productive. He allowed some private farms and businesses, hoping that the Soviet workers would take more pride and care in their jobs.

Perestroika had other effects too. In the Baltics and other dissatisfied Soviet states, Gorbachev relaxed the rules prohibiting the use of native languages. And festivals and native customs that were once forbidden by Moscow could be enjoyed by the Baltic people.

But the most drastic change had to do with the Baltics nations' calls for freedom. Gorbachev announced that any republic that wished to break away had that right. He urged the states *not* to leave the Soviet Union, however, and hoped that his new policies of openness would make people willing to remain part of it.

Mikhail Gorbachev

The Unraveling Begins

Gorbachev's words were greeted with joy by the Baltic people. He became a symbol of hope for them. Newspapers in Latvia, Lithuania and Estonia called him "a man of vision." By 1987 he was actually more popular in the Baltics than in the republic of Russia, his native home!

And the Baltic people took his words seriously. Estonians formed the Popular Front of Estonia in 1988. This organization called for more freedom in the economy, urged democratic elections, and pushed for Estonian to replace Russian as its state's official language.

Latvia and Lithuania too organized to make sweeping changes in their republics. People held rallies and waved their native flags. Gorbachev's hope—that if he offered the Baltics the right to leave, they wouldn't—was beginning to backfire. Talk of independence was growing louder and more fervent in all three of the Baltic states.

The Baltic Way

The most powerful statement of hope in the Baltics occurred on August 23, 1989, the 50th anniversary of the pact between Stalin and Hitler. An estimated one million Balts joined hands. They formed a human chain that stretched 400 miles through all three capitals, Vilnius, Tallinn and Riga.

"It is called the Baltic Way," said an 18-year-old student who participated. "It is the most beautiful feeling I ever had. The power of the Baltic people could be felt, hand to hand, one to another."

Another member of the chain agreed. "It is impossible for me to believe that so many people could want something so pure, so necessary, and not get it," he said. "Freedom is so basic, and the Baltic Way has sent that message to the world."

A Lithuanian joins in a mass protest calling for Soviet withdrawal from the Baltics.

The Return of the Hard Line

But the reaction from Moscow and Gorbachev was far different from what the members of the Baltic Way expected. The Soviet leader warned the Baltic people that they were "in danger of crossing a line that they best not cross." It was a threat—and the Baltic people knew it.

But they chose to ignore the threat. The Lithuanians unanimously voted for independence on March 11, 1990. They pulled down the Soviet flag in their parliament and hoisted the Lithuanian flag as thousands gathered to cheer. Many older people who remembered the injustices of the past wiped tears of joy from their faces.

Latvia and Estonia followed Lithuania's lead. They were more open-ended than Lithuania, however. They were firm about wanting their independence but set no specific dates for it to take effect.

The reaction from Moscow was angry. There was to be no breaking away, said the Soviet leader. Any republic leaving the Soviet Union would have to follow a strict procedure. It would take months, perhaps years, to work out a settlement that was fair to both sides. Certainly it could not happen overnight.

Gorbachev also reminded the Balts that not all the Soviet leaders in Moscow were as liberal as he. Some of them were hard-line Communists, in the tradition of Stalin. Gorbachev warned the Baltic people that he could not always control the hard-liners, who might want to punish any breakaway republics.

A young woman holds a sign outside the Latvian parliament on the day the last Baltic state declared independence.

The message was clear: The people of the Baltics must take back their independence notices at once or suffer the consequences.

The Baltic people were furious. They called Gorbachev "a typical Communist liar, no better than Stalin or Lenin." One newspaper editor admitted that Gorbachev was perhaps more charming than the other Communists of the past, "but underneath, he smells just as false."

Lines form for gasoline, after Gorbachev cut off energy sources to the Baltics.

Lithuanians stand firm against a Soviet tank, one of many that tried to seize control of the elected government.

Bloodshed in the Baltics

None of the three republics would back down, however. And Moscow carried through on its threats. First, Soviet troops arrived in the Baltics. Bloodshed followed soon, as protesters were beaten by soldiers. A Lithuanian hospital that was protecting independence leaders was stormed and many people were injured. A U.S. television crew was there, recording the incident. Soviet soldiers demanded that the video be handed over to them.

Next, shipments of natural gas and oil were cut off to the Baltics. Winter was fast approaching, and the people knew that they did not have enough energy sources to supply their own heat. Without Soviet supplies, they would freeze.

Leaders of the independence movement were reluctant to give in. When Moscow cut off energy sources, homes and businesses in the Baltics suffered. Finally, Baltic leaders agreed to slow down in their demands. However, they did repeat their intentions to work hard at hammering out an agreement with Moscow that would give them freedom.

Thousands gather to show their determination to be free.

Black Berets attempt to attack the government buildings in Lithuania.

"It Is Now Time"

But Moscow was dragging its feet on the agreement. As months went by with little progress for independence for the Baltics, frustration grew. As the Baltic people became angrier, tension between them and the Soviet soldiers stationed there increased too.

In January 1991, Soviet soldiers attacked a television station in Vilnius, Lithuania. They wanted to take control of the station, which they felt was "fueling the drive for independence in the Baltics." In the bloody attack, 15 people were killed. A similar attack followed in Latvia.

A young woman leads a funeral procession for a man killed by Soviet troops.

Normally, the people of the world would hear of such an action, and would have reacted with anger toward the Soviets. The world's attention, however, was focused not on the Baltics but on the Persian Gulf, where war had just broken out. Many of the governments around the world were critical of Moscow's actions, but little was done to condemn them formally.

The end came just months afterward. After a failed coup in Moscow, the Soviet Union seemed ready for collapse. In the confusion following the coup, there was little Gorbachev or anyone else could do to stop the Baltics from breaking away.

"It is now time," one Soviet official said. "There is no reason to stop them now."

FREEDOM, WITH A PRICE

The granting of independence to the Baltic states was not an automatic happy ending to their story. In fact, for many Baltic people, the real struggle is just beginning.

Gorbachev formally recognizes the freedom of the Baltic states.

A Ruined Economy

A great deal must be changed in Lithuania, Latvia and Estonia if the countries are going to survive. The most important issue is their economies.

Not one of the Baltic states is self-sufficient. Years of communism have left their economies intertwined with those of other Soviet states. The Baltics lack raw materials from which to produce factory items, as well as energy and fuel.

When they were part of the Soviet Union, of course, they could barter for these materials. Fuel and energy were purchased at cut-rate prices. But now the Soviets have no reason to give the Baltic people deals. Experts estimate that fuel alone will cost Lithuania over $700 million each year—$700 million more than it has to spend.

"Where Do We Belong Now?"

Another important problem is the population makeup of the Baltic states. No longer are the vast majority of people Lithuanian, Estonian or Latvian. There are many Russians who have made their homes in the Baltics.

"I came here in 1961," said a Russian who works as a banker in Estonia. "I like the country, and I have always felt a part of this place; it is my home. But there is much talk here of getting rid of traitors and Russians. Does that mean I am not welcome?"

A Russian schoolteacher from Latvia voiced similar feelings. "I have had hateful notes sent to me, and my children have been called bad names," she says sadly. "I voted for freedom in the elections because I thought it was right. I thought I understood the people here, but maybe I was wrong. If not here, then where is it that I belong?"

Many Baltic people insist that they have no quarrel with Russians who live in their countries. They say that they will not discriminate against Russians in housing or jobs, even though they themselves have been discriminated against. Baltic leaders have said that to become strong members of the world community they will need help from *all* their people, not just those of Baltic heritage.

"We Are Like a Newborn Child"

For the people of the Baltics, there is joy but also a feeling of being behind. The coup gave them the opportunity for freedom that they had been looking for, but it came sooner than they had planned.

"We are still halfway in the door of the Soviet Union," says a Lithuanian government worker. "For instance, any letter going to another country automatically is sent to Moscow. The post offices there take care of it eventually—in three or four months.

"The same is true for telephone calls. The overseas switchboards are in Moscow. If I want to call my niece in the United States, I have to register for the call about a week ahead of time. We are very slow here, but when we can handle our own communication, we'll be better off."

A group of Lithuanians show the victory sign.

A member of the Estonian parliament is confident that with the help and aid of the rest of the world, the Baltics will get on their feet soon. It's just that freedom came so suddenly, she says.

"We are like a newborn child who arrived unexpectedly in the seventh month," she explains. "We have to do things quickly so that we can survive in this new environment."

In the months to come, the world will be watching to see how well the Baltic people are surviving with their new freedom.

FACTS ABOUT THE BALTIC STATES

Estonia

Capital: Tallinn

Population: 1.6 million

Form of government: democracy

Resources: timber, oil

Official Language: Estonian, Russian

Latvia

Capital: Riga

Population: 2.7 million

Form of government: democracy

Resources: amber, peat

Official Language: Latvian, Russian

Lithuania

Capital: Vilnius

Population: 3.8 million

Form of government: democracy

Resources: timber, peat, amber

Official Language: Lithuanian, Russian

Glossary

archaeologists *People who study the remains of ancient civilizations.*

collective *A large farm in a Communist country, managed by government workers.*

communism *An economic system based on the idea that all people should share wealth equally. All businesses and property are owned by the state.*

coup *A military takeover of a government.*

czar *A Russian emperor.*

glasnost *A Russian term meaning "openness."*

guerrilla war *Military actions carried out by a small force with the object of harassing the enemy, interrupting its lines of communication and destroying its supplies.*

perestroika *A restructuring of the Soviet government introduced by Mikhail Gorbachev, the former Soviet premier.*

serfs *Poor people who worked for rich landowners during the Middle Ages.*

Index